I HEAR YOU NOW!

*God Is Love/God Is Our Conscience/
God makes the world go around*

Carla Sweat

authorHOUSE

AuthorHouse™
1663 Liberty Drive
Bloomington, IN 47403
www.authorhouse.com
Phone: 833-262-8899

*This book is a work of non-fiction. Unless otherwise noted, the author and the publisher make
no explicit guarantees as to the accuracy of the information contained in this book and in some
cases, names of people and places have been altered to protect their privacy.*

Published by AuthorHouse 08/20/2020

ISBN: 978-1-4259-2571-0 (sc)

Library of Congress Control Number: 2006902200

Print information available on the last page.

This book is printed on acid-free paper.

DEDICATED TO THE ONE I LOVE:

My inspirator, David my love, I could not of done what I wanted in my life if it was not for you. You have put your trust in me, and I have cherished it all the way. You are the one who holds the Key to my Kingdom. You are the one who has carried us thou all things. Thank you God. Who I have trusted all my days. Thank you Jesus, for David's being *baptized in union with you* (Col. 1:15).

For myself, I still have *a baptism to go to*, and will be distressed until I get there. *Luke 12:50*. Although for now I accurately know the truth, I best be hurrying up to get to my baptism. This is a sin to know and not act upon for this I know. God knows I am not here to baptize but to spread his God News of the Kingdom. Let it be preached. Thank you Lord for my promised wedding bliss, which I have received wholeheartedly. Now I need my salvation to God's Kingdom in heaven for everlasting life. Not obtainable through mankind only through Christ Jesus our Lord and Master. There is only one true Jehovah God who gave us his only begotten son Jesus Christ our Lord and Savior. Thank you David for being my faithful witness, who God has loved. Thank you for the years of hard labour I have put you through. Our love is like a match made in heaven a waiting to be lit in order to start a blazing fire, all for heaven made.

ACT 13:26

men and brethren, sons of the family of Abraham, and those among you who fear God to use the word of this salvation has been sent.

Revelations 19:1

after these things I heard a loud voice of a great multitude in heaven, saying" Alleluia, salvation and glory and honor and power to the Lord our God.

Revelations 19 :9

then he said to me, "write : blessed are those who were called to the marriage supper of the lamb! And he said to me these are the true sayings of God."

I HEAR YOU NOW!

Hebrews 13:4

Marriage is honourable in all, and the bed undefiled: but whoremongers and adulterers God will judge. 8.2.5.6.9

II Corinthians 11:2

For I am jealous over you with godly jealousy: for I have espoused you to one husband, that I may present you as a chaste virgin to Christ. 8.2.5.6.7.

Matthew 24:45 – 51

Who really is the faithful and discreet slave whom his master appointed over his domestils, to give them their food at the proper time? Happy is that slave if his master on arriving finds him doing so. Truly I say to you, He will appoint him over all his belonging. 8.2.4.6.7

Matthew 27:29 – 65

And they braided a crown out of thorns and put it on his head and a reed in his right hand. 9.2.5.6.8.

Matthew 27:33, 37

And when they came to a place called Gol-go-tha, that is to say, skull place. 9.2.5.6.8.

Also, they pasted above his head the charge against him in writing: *This is Jesus the King of the Jews.* 9.2.5.6.8.

Mark 15:22

So they brought him to the place Gol' go-tha, which means when translated, Skull Place. 9.2.5.6.8.

Mark 15:26

And the inscription of the charge against him was written above, *The King Of The Jews.* 9.2.5.6.8.

Luke 23:33

And when they got to the place called skull, there they impaled him and the evil doers, one on his right and one on his left. 9.2.5.6.8.

Daniel 7:9.13.21

I kept on beholding until there were thrones placed the Ancient of Days sat down. His clothing was White just like snow, and the hair of his head was like clean wool. His throne was flames of fire; it wheels were a burning fire. 9.2.5.6.8.

I kept on beholding in the visions of the night and see there: with the clouds of the heavens someone like a son of man happened to be coming; and to the Ancient of Days he gained access, and they brought him up close even before that One. 9.2.5.6.8.

And to him there were given rulership and dignity and kingdom, that the peoples, national groups, and languages should all serve even him. His rulership is an indefinitely lasting rulership that will not pass away, and his Kingdom one that will not be brought to ruin. 9.2.5.6.8.

This is true, for this comes from the house of David.

Daniel 7:9.13.15.22.28

As for me, Daniel, my spirit was distressed within on account of it, and the very visions of my head began to frighten me. 9.2.5.6.8.

Until the Ancient of Days come, and judgment itself was given in favor of the holy ones of the Supreme One, and the definite time arrived that the holy ones took possession of the Kingdom itself. 9.2.5.6.8.

Up to this point is the end of the matter. As for me, Daniel, my own thoughts kept frightening me a great deal, so that my very complexion changed in me, but the matter itself I kept in my own heart. 9.2.5.6.8.

The Ancients Are Wise And Good

For now we see through a glass darkly, but they altar, now I know in "part, but then shall I know even as also I am known." 9.2.5.6.8.

CONTENTS

GOD IS LOVE

Psalms 119:1.1.10

Happy are the ones faultless in [their] way. The ones walking in the law of Jehovah.

Happy are those observing his reminders; with all the heart they keep searching for him. 9.2.5.6.8.

With my whole heart I have searched for you. 9.2.5.6.8.

St. Matthew 13:9 – 17

Let him that has ears listen. 9.2.5.6.8.

St. Matthew 13:17 – 19

For verily I say unto you, That many prophets and righteous men have desired to those things which ye see, and have not seen them, and to hear those things which ye hear, and have not heard them. 8.2.5.6.9

Whosoever cometh to me, and heareth my sayings and doeth them, I will show you to whom he is like.

St. John 5:39 – 47

Search the Scriptures, for in them ye think ye have eternal life: and they are they which testify of me 8.2.5.6.9.

Or

St. John 5:39 – 47

You are searching the Scriptures, because you think that by means of them you will have everlasting life; and these are the very ones that bear witness about me. 9.2.5.6.8.

I HEAR YOU NOW

"Let the Good News of God's Kingdom be Preached" (PS68:11, Isa. 43:10-12, Matt. 24:14, Rev. 14:6-8). We must be living in the times of it. The time to preach his great name (PS. 118:24). "I am Jehovah" (Isaiah 42:8). "Don't be afraid" (Isa.43:1). "It is indefinitely (John 17:3). "Fear only God" (PS 33:8). "I am Alpha and Omega, the beginning and the end" (Rev. 1:8). Faith it is to time indeed. "It is because I have always believed in him above. He is the saviour of all men, especially of those that believe. Because of evil times" (Thess. 1-10). "Jesus said, except ye see signs and wonders, ye will not believe" (St. John 4:48). "I have also spoken by the prophets and I have multiplied visions and used similitudes by the ministry of the prophets" (Hosea 12:10). "John indeed baptized with water; but he shall be baptized with the Holy Ghost" (Acts 11:16).

All scriptures are quoted from one or the other five sources of references listed. Please feel free to use your own source on hand. There is only one true God, and he serves all of us the same.

There are many things I have to say about my God while preaching the Good News of His Kingdom. For starters, the truth I have no reason to lie. He is all good. Thank you for our parents, immediate family, family friends, and health. There is no need to see him. It has always been within. He has always been there for me. He has always been there. Autism with no medication or diagnosis but with his sound of mind. Nursing licenses, writing, wisdom, pleasures, joy, life, and death.

I thank you for the many splendor of things that you have given me for I am not worthy. For only you and I know for what I ask for. I must say I have what I have deserved. The list can go on, but there are lessons to be learned.

Lesson One: I must tell all. I tell you this story because I have come to an end of the road. I have never been ashamed of myself before now. I am having to face the realities surrounding me. The peace of mind that I once possess – I want to challenge. Slightly out of boredom and fear. See, I have to be honest. I was taught better so I knew better. I was brought up by my God given mother and the love of my grandmother.

I was taught on how to please my maker, but I let the devil in. I let down my guard, so I stopped minding my thoughts. Now I need redemption and God has always been my only way out. I have fallen and I cannot get up. I am in the bottomless pit. The Lord is the only way to cast my demons out. Salvation is what I need, and God's mercy, grace, and loving kindness is the answer. The times are more critical than ever because the devil is out. He takes control of people, the ones that do not serve the Lord. God knows; so go to him, so the devil does not take control of your soul. The times are being fulfilled as promised. We are just living the times.

LOVE IS WHAT MAKES
THE WORLD GO AROUND

Repent, and turn back our wicked ways. God is at hand. Jehovah God sent his only begotten son Jesus Christ, our Saviour and Master to bear our sins. Our times are short and getting shorter.

If we stay on our Master's path, he will show us the way. Hopefully, we can be used along the way. I am living my dream. Never be afraid to dream because God is our dream. He helps us get there, but not alone. God is love, there is nothing else in between. The Kingdom is at hand, and I am here to preach the "Good News of God's Kingdom Let It Be Preached." (Matthew 24:14)

In loving memories of our departed: Grandparents, in-laws, nephews, and cousins. We love you and will always be thinking about you.

Parents, I am thankful for my parents; just for the simple fact of being able to say they are here, alive and well. Although my biological father left my mother and family after ten years of marriage, I still need his loving thoughts and prayers. Five years ago, I tried again to contact my father in order to invite him to our daughter's wedding.

Well, she got hold of him on the phone and tried to invite him to the wedding. Before she could even say the date, he stated he was too busy that day. This is all I have to say about my biological father. Besides, my mother loved him too much if you ask me, but who is asking? My mother does all she can to make up the difference. It still hurts, only because the family's proceedings use; had only more wealth that he was searching. Dad called her up on the telephone just to say that they were divorced from Mexico. No questions asked. Moma raised five girls with the lost of one twin. I do believe she is enjoying life because she is a Jehovah Witness who is taught on how to live in this forsaken world. Not that she is above problems or no, but the devil does not slip in unexpected.

My mother took us all to the Kingdom Hall faithful whether we wanted to go or not. I use to put up a fight sometimes, but it always ended up worthwhile. I was brought up in the Kingdom Hall as a babe (Matthew 11:25). Although I acted out on my mother by rebellion, I remembered Jesus promised to take care of us if our parents would just give us to him. Story has it, my biological father again, tells my mother to get into the Jehovah Witness organization. I personally try not to be hurt over his loss, because my heavenly father has taken better care of us. My Lord has fulfilled my impossibilities. My biological dad could only hope and pray for my impossibilities. God be with you: As I sit listening to the meetings at The Kingdom Hall I would always wonder why? I would hear a voice inside of me talking and telling me good things to hear during those times the bible was being read. I hear you now Lord, loud and clear, just as before. I just did not want to listen then, but I tried. Never well enough for this I know. All of my sisters were baptized as witness but not me.

Mark 10:19

Honor your Father and Mother. 9.2.5.6.8

Three of my sisters which happen to be the oldest were baptized early in there lives. So she stopped the baptisms and left it up to my younger sister and I. I have yet to get baptized. I know better but I have always believed and was afraid of getting baptized in the truth. Now I know. I know which I always did. I was just afraid. Now I am hoping to still be able to get in. The truth will set you free.

Mark 10:13

Now people began bringing him young children for him to touch these; but the disciples reprimand them. 9.2.5.6.8.

GOD IS OUR CONSCIENCE

God has always been within.

God is our conscience, and I wear mine on my shoulder. So I free myself from a lot of worries by putting all and what I do, so my conscience comes first.

Lesson to Learn. Help myself and others too. What do I have to say? As I said before, the truth for starters. Let me begin by saying, this book is to bear true testimony for the believers. The believers in Praises to Jehovah God and Jesus Christ His only begotten Son our Savior. The non-believers, critics or skeptics are not of my concern only because I can only do so much. I am here to tell you about some of the miracle events, wonders, and signs that have happened in my life. God does not lie.

My husband is the joy in my life. I was 15 years old when I met my husband in high school. Although we both lived in the projects I had never seen him before. I will never forget the first time we met. It was while in school. I was walking past the yellow lockers while he stands with a friend. He said to me, "Hey, youi chasti Morgan." I turned and smiled. There was a time when my body was built and fit. The time before our kids.

It was not long after that we had begun to date. I trusted David then and still do. I knew no other boys just a lot of friends. David betrayed our trust first then I followed. Not before I first got pregnant at the age of 15. David and I went our separate ways for a while. We were back together within two years, but not before he escaped without having another child by someone who also confessed loving him.

Lesson Learned: I broke my promise to God when I first had sex before intent by wedding plans. I was ashamed of being an unwed mother. God was still with me, he helped me along the way. He gave me the intrinsic ability to bear and raise a child at my young age. God is good; he gave me the insight to be a good parent. I was not ready or prepared mindfully, spiritually, or financially for that type of life-long responsibility. As always, trusting in the Lord led me through it. I believe my life would of went smoother in all things if I just would of listened when He told me. I say "smoother" because the important issues I now face with my husband would not of been. I know this because I married a fellow not knowing the truth. The truth as I know it. We have the same God but beliefs are different.

I know we can make it with God being the leader, but we both have to learn how to listen to him. I know because God tells me to work on my marriage for this is his world. I am always trying to please my God. There has never been a greater man than John the Baptist.

Lesson Learned: The time I became of legal age to get married without parental consent we did. I can remember being nervous because my body broke out in hives on the way to the justice of the peace. The day went good although it was gloomy looking outside. I just knew our plans were ruined only because of some misty rain. It all went well that day. I have a saying; since that day, It is raining on the outside but not in the inside. The saying still holds true for me today. The only difference is I now know the significance of the rain. "God is the holder of rain." (I King 18:1 – 2)

Lesson Learned: God is still with us – Alive as always. Knowing our every move. Let me tell you this short story. It was on a clear day not long ago while outside in the yard. David and I were fooling around cleaning up the outside. I said to him, "It smells like rain." He replied, "Oh no!" I had suggested to put up the car windows. Believe it or not it rained not too much later that day. Not hard, just enough to notice and tell David to look outside then it stopped. David replied, "Good for you." God works in mysterious ways, and I am not made to wonder. All hearts belong to God. He allows us to surrender our hearts. If we do not he waits until we call him. For you may think it is for yourself, really it has always been his. Our maker and Savior all in Jesus name.

Shortly after being married for a short time we had our first son. Even though David had his first son before our marriage it was God's will David's other son is a part of our life but he is not in our life. I must say David did try to make him a part of our life but it takes two.

Our daughter and son are all grown up now. My, where did the time go? I must say I have always been inpatient. What I now realize is it was always there. I just needed to learn to be more patient.

Our children are all grown up now. I say, where did the time go? Our first child is off and married happily. The last one yet to go. Shawntal, our daughter, and Micah our son-in-law are presently proud parents to five beautiful boys. Micah, Jr. being eight and the oldest one. The ages ranging from three, two, and six months with a couple of twins. All are healthy and good kids. Our children, I carried in my heart our grandkids touch my heart. When a three year old child say something out of the blues from there heart it sounds like songs of words needed to touch your heart. I was beginning to feel useless; when it comes to whether or not my involvement so closely was necessary or even needed to a certain extent. Today, like always I get the answers to the question that is apparently bothering me. Sweet sounding words helps you move forward positively. Sour ones stop you in your tracks, and makes you think sad. I do not have to say much to our daughter about life and serving God. The reason being is she already knows. Our daughter followed after my footsteps and became a nurse as well. Shawntal enjoys caring for people, well or sick.

My stepson, that is all I can say let the truth be known. I know in my heart for some reason or another I always wanted a mixed child. I did not know how or why but I did. He is not in our life but a part of our life. I must say, that years ago when he was on my mind a vision of him appeared in my mind. Just to say he is okay. The fact of the matter is, he has a mother that loves him and has cared for him. He did call us one day as an adult, and called me mother. I was touched, so my feelings paid off.

My broken promise to our son. When I do not see the evidence of God's present I always know it is the consciousness that holds the guilty. Guilt for the wrong done in an circumstances. Wrong you know you are guilty of. That is no fun to any degree. I rather not have the guilt. I felt guilty when I changed my mind to help him out of his situation because I did forewarn him. David, Jr. is going to be 22 years old in about eight more days and he is still under our roof. I am thankful he is a good child. I want only the best for both of our kids – David, Sr.'s other child too, we want only what is best.

A broken promise to myself, I must admit I am guilty. Guilty of not listening to my Lord at first. I hear you now Lord. I did not realize what I was really asking for until now. I must have been asking for it. The shadow of death, has passed me by, soon to be back, and my only shield is the Lord (I King 19:11). I have asked for something that will cause my death forever. Little did I want to realize what He has always said and meant. Now I know and I would be stupid to search for it. Only tho my salvation will God help me now. I have confessed to knowing. Baptized or not baptized it is a sin to ignore God's commands. I have been a party to lawlessness, and have lost self-control. Thou God's mercy and grace I ask for your loving kindness to see me thou. I battle with the number one War Good versus Evil and Love-n-hate. For the love of God's Kingdom and the hate of any other.

Sacred Holy Grounds I call it because I witnessed a miracle take place. It was the "invisible image of God's first borne of all creation." (Genesis 2:7). I was around the age of twelve when I was shown this miracle. I stepped outside my backyard in the projects and where no grass had ever grown. The dust from the ground began to rise up right in a perfect whirlwind dirt pattern position just like an image of a thunder wave pattern.

I was amazed, to say the least. I remember there was no breeze blowing to of caused such a force of action. This was for my eyes only. No one else to of witnessed just me. Now, being God's faithful witness, I am allowed to preach God's Good News of His Kingdom.

And in them is fulfilled the prophets of Esaias, which saith, by having ye shall hear, and shall not understand; and seeing ye shall, and shall not perceive. 9.2.5.6.8.

Lesson to learn: The manifested event of this miracle took place in the inner east side of the Bluegrass Aspendale Projects. This was 30 years ago, and there has been no changes made in this area at all. People now call it Bluegrass Aspendale East End Drug Infectious Projects. This inner part of East End projects is the only standing areas left to be torn down. The remaining projects are either already broken grounds since the state of development. "What is left still remaining of a drug infected community." The people stand outside and promote lawlessness.

The lawman do not even drive by anymore. A statement from a friend who states, "We don't have to worry about them." Apparently they think they are their friends only while it suits them. I say, the rest will be discovered.

St. Mark 14:8,9 + 62

She hath done what she could: She is come aforehand to anoint my body to the burying. 6.2.5.8.9

Verily I say unto you. Whersoever this gospel shall be preached throughout the whole world, this also that she hath done shall be spoken of for a memorial of her. 6.2.6.8.9.

I am: and ye shall see the Son of man sitting on the right hand of power, and coming in the clouds of heaven. 9.2.5.6.8.

St. Mark 16:15 – 18 + 19 – 20

Go ye into all the world, and preach the gospel of every creature. 9.2.5.6.8

He that believeth and is baptized shall be saved; but he that believeth not shall be damned. 9.2.5.6.8.

And these signs shall follow them that believe: In my name shall they cast our devils; they shall speak with new tongues. 9.2.5.6.8.

They shall take up serpents; and if they drink any deadly thing it shall not hurt them, they shall lay hands on the sick and they shall recover. 9.2.5.6.8.

LOVE IS WHAT MAKES
THE WORLD GO ROUND

Lesson Learned: I once again found myself in the presence of a Higher Being. During another situation, I all of a sudden felt a gentle constant breeze of wind come upon me. This experience felt like an out body miracle event. I was conscious the whole time during this event. The feeling was weightless. I remember selfishly wishing it could of lasted longer. This experience was only given from above, heavenly divine. My body felt the regeneration and renewing of the Holy Ghost. During this same time period, after the releasing of the Holy Spirit felt from my body, I experienced my soul living me from inside my body, from my head to straight down through my toes. It felt weird. I tried to shake it off when I felt it at my toes. The event before the soul left I was touched with the presence of God. I say that because I turned to my right side when He sounded and low and behold was the presence of a large white star bright and beautiful. I watched in amazement. The presence of several other stars twinkling around just as clear as day. White and gold aura all around this beautiful color of matrixes.

Titus 3:5 – 8

Not by works of righteousness, which we have done, but according to his mercy he saved us, by the washing of regeneration, and renewing of the Holy Ghost. 8.9.2.5.6.

Which he shed on us abundantly though Jesus Christ our Saviour. 5.2.6.8.9.

I must also say, personally I do believe we are marked by our body – The term birthmark. I wear the marking of a cloud at my right foot. Our daughter has the marking of the raindrop on her body. She has it on her face – as if she was crying, crying raindrops.

2 Corinthians 12:1 – 10

I have to brag. There is nothing to be gained by it, but I must brag about the visions and other things that the Lord has shown me. I know about one of Christ's followers who was taken up into the third heaven fourteen years ago. I don't know if the man was still in his body when it happened, but God certainly knows.

As I said, only God really knows if this man was in his body at the time. But he was taken up into paradise, where he heard things that are too wonderful to tell. I will brag about that man, but not about myself, except to say how weak I am. Yet even if I did brag,

I would not be foolish. I would simply be speaking the truth. But I will try not to say too much. That way, none of you will think more highly of me than you should because of what you have seen me do and say. Of course, I am now referring to the wonderful things I saw. One of Satan's angels was sent to make me suffer terribly, so that I would not feel too proud. Three times I begged the Lord to make this suffering go away. But re replied, "My kindness is all you need. My power is strongest when you are weak." So if Christ keeps giving me his power, I will gladly brag about how weak I am. Yes, I am glad to be weak or insulted or mistreated or to have troubles and sufferings, if it is for Christ. Because when I am weak I am strong. 2.5.6.8.9.

Lesson to Learn: The reason; why the shadow of death was upon me is because I had no business being out in the midnight hours. As I said before he is always with us. Jesus left us his comforter. I have always believed. It was midnight and I just got home from work. I decided to walk to the mailbox because of the midnight air feeling good. Although it was past 2:30 a.m., I just was not thinking. I am never afraid like I should be. I trust people and I know God. The very good thing is he knows me. I should have been thinking about my family at home who of course were sleeping. That would have been an isolated event that could of happened to me. Instead, God let me know I was not along. All of a sudden while walking down the hill to the mailbox, I heard a light noise to my left. I turned and saw just as clear as day an odd shape figure that was black in color. And laid on top of the green grass between some trees. Then once I noticed the odd black shaped figure I watched it move slow, quick before my eyes (I King 19:11). I could not stop thinking about that odd shape I saw and what was all of that about. The time passed and I decided to draw that figure so distinctly seen on a piece of paper. Once I drew the figure I was shocked at how much that it looked like the right side of a hand. The size was as large as the shadow of the trees. It was hard for me to believe, until God explained what I saw.

Luke 22:53

While I was with you in the temple day after day you did not stretch out your hand against me, but this is your hour and the authority of darkness.

Hebrews 9:24 – 28

For Christ entered, not into a holy place made with hands, which is a copy of the reality, but into heaven itself, now to appear before the person of God for us. 9.2.5.6.8.

Otherwise, he would have to suffer often from the founding of the world. But now has manifested himself once for all time at the conclusion of the systems of things to put sin away through the sacrifice for men to die once for all time, but after this a judgment, so also the Christ was offered once for all time to bear the sins of man; and the second time that he appears it will be apart from sin and to those earnestly looking for him for [their] salvation. 9.2.5.6.8.

Hebrews 10:1 – 39, Chap: 11, 12, 13

For since the Law has a shadow of the good things to come, but not the very substance of the things [men] can never with the same sacrifices from year to year which they offer continually make those who approach perfect. 9.2.5.6.8.

...then he actually says, "Look! I am come to do your will." He does away with what is first that he may establish what is second. By the said "will" we have been sanctified through the offering of the body of Jesus Christ once for all time. 9.2.5.6.8.

Hebrews 10:15

Moreover, the holy spirit also bears witness to us, for after it has said. 9.2.5.6.8.

[It says afterwards] And I shall by no means call their sins and their lawless deeds to mind anymore. Now where there is forgiveness of these, there is no longer an offering for sin. Therefore, brothers, since we have boldness for the way of entry into the holy place by the blood of Jesus, let us approach with true hearts in the full assurance of faith, having had our hearts sprinkled from a wicked conscience and our bodies bathed with clean water. Let us hold fast the public declaration of our hope without wavering for he is faithful that promised. 9.2.5.6.8.

Now that I know the truth, I am held accountable for all accurate knowledge of the truth. God has shown me enough of his glory to stand still or walk straight into his glory to last me my life time.

St. John 4:48

However, Jesus said to him: Unless you people see signs and wonders, you will by no means believe. 9.2.5.6.8.

St. Matthew 12:38, 39

Then as an answer to him some of the scribes and Pharisees said: "Teacher, we want to see a sign from you." In reply he said to them: "A wicked and adulterous generation keeps on seeking for a sign, but no sign will be given it except the sign of Jo'nah the prophet." 9.2.5.6.8.

St. Matthew 11:20

Then he stated to reproach the cities in which most of his powerful works had taken place, because they did not repent. 9.2.5.6.8.

John 5:31 – 38

If I alone bear witness about myself, my witness is not true. There is another that bears witness about me, and I know that the witness which he bears about me is true. You have dispatched men to John, and he had borne witness to the truth. However, I do not accept the witness from man, but I say these things that you may be saved. But I have the witness greater than that of John, for the very works that my Father assigned me to accomplish, the works themselves that I am doing, bear witness about me that the Father dispatched me. Also, the Father who sent me has himself borne witness about me. You have neither heard his voice at any time nor seen his figure, and you do not have his word remaining in you, because the very one whom he dispatched you do not believe. 9.2.5.6.8.

John: 40 + 44 – 47

For this is the will of my Father, that everyone that beholds the Son and exercises faith in him should have everlasting life, and I will resurrect him out the last day. 9.2.5.6.8.

No man can come to me unless the Father, who sent me, draws him; and I will resurrect him in the last day. It is written in Prophets, and they will all be taught by Jehovah. Everyone that has heard from the Father and has learned comes to me. Not that any man has seen the father, except he who is from God; this one has seen the Father. Most truly I say to you, He that believes has everlasting life. 9.2.5.6.8.

John 4:24, 26 – 28

God is a spirit, and those worshiping him must worship with spirit and truth. Jesus said to her, "I who am speaking to you am he." Now at this point his disciples arrived, and they began to wonder because he was speaking with a woman. Of course no one said: "What are you looking for?" or, "Why do you talk with her?" The woman, therefore, left her water jar and went off into the city and told the men: 9.2.5.6.8.

Now I will continue on with the Shadows description:

Hebrews 11:19

Accounting that God was able to raise him up, even from the dead from whence also he received him in a figure. 9.2.5.6.8.

I King 18:44

"Look! There is a small cloud like a man's palm ascending out of the sea." 9.2.5.6.8.

For now, do you understand what I mean when I say that Jehovah, my God has always been with me. Description have it his very hand has proven to be upon me. The right hand as you can see, by God's anatomy. "And, look; Jehovah was passing by" (I King 19:11).

The time is now and the Kingdom of God is at hand: repent ye and believe the gospel.

St. Mark 16:15

Go ye into all the world, and preach the gospel to every creature. 9.2.5.6.8.

St. Luke 4:43

I must preach the Kingdom of God to other cities also: for therefore am I sent. 9.2.5.6.8.

St. Matthew 13:57

A prophet is not without honour, save in his own country, and in his own house. 2.5.6.8.9.

Philemon 1:8

For this very reason, though I have great freeness of speech in connection with Christ to order you to do what is proper. 9.2.5.6.8.

GOD IS OUR CONSCIENCE
WHETHER WE USE HIM OR NOT

In my personal public opinion my issues are why are the inner eastside project still standing? Badly representing Lexington's lawlessness were there need not be. As I mentioned before, the only remaining old projects still standing are where I lived at 30 years ago. *David* and I both, his area as well as mine. This area is small compared to others. The plan was to rebuild the project but for some reason or another the plans were dropped. The agenda needs to be reviewed. The funding that was either lost or stolen needs to be refunded. The process needs to move on. The reputation is bad. Now called Drug Infectious East End Bluegrass Aspendall Projects. When this Lexington lawyer mother ask me about this slope of the Projects I was too quick to respond. I guess I did not want to believe it. So after doing some investigation I found it to be true. Even the state and government agents regarded the Projects as infected with drugs. I wonder why. Our people do not have the financial resources to keep this type of community a flowing. This is the work of the devil, preying on the poor. We are guilty but not by ourselves. The people have lost their faith. So I hope I put faith there where there is none to visualize. Otherwise the people are doomed. It is already out of control. People are allowed to traffic illegal drugs without being stopped from law officers of any kind.

The time is now because the end is here. If we repent with our heart, soul, body, and mind God may forgive us. I believe my Lord, for he has promised. Of course, we have to do our part whole-heartedly otherwise, the channel to connect is not there. People, we are a party to the lawlessness if we watch out for the under dogs. This system of things is almost over and we are running out of time. You know it and I know it. For it is only a matter of time. God is at hand and his passing me by. I confess my time is up and it is over. People, this is my letter of salvation. I did not know this was how it was going to go down. Yes, I was told, but I did not want to believe. Now that death is upon me, like it is for all, I better let God help me along the way. And hope that there is still time. Not for me to see, just for me to act upon. God know when you know, and he holds us accountable when you know. Do not you people wait to see. Repent and save yourself. For the time is near, God is at hand. The Good News of God's Kingdom I am preaching. Turn from our wicked ways, so the devil has to turn away. I know the devil tries as hard as you do just to keep us on our toes. He will stop when he falls because he does not stand upright. But you do because God stands us upright with him. Stop the devil in his tracks and he will fall.

The west side of town where I resided with my grandmother for a period of time looks better because that job was completed and filled with outrages prices for mortgages. Why? When the ground are the same. There is a problem with drugs across the street where mortgage prices are dropped. Run by the same organization as the East side projects, one side of the street, but not the other. People allowed to lofty around and practice lawlessness. I even hear inside source say, Winburn area has gotten even bad.

The North and South side are just as bad, but crime is done in the house with two, three witness outside to be a party to the lawlessness.

It has to be a change and a spirit change at that. The world is doomed. God is our only way out. Pray for God to deliver us from sin and change our wicked ways. Jesus is waiting on us but not for long. The time is now.

I am a former student of the University of Kentucky. I attended briefly. I graduated from the Lexington Community College with a two-year degree, and completed courses at several of the Technical Colleges around town. I also attended Eastern University, and enjoyed other courses needed for education. I must say illegal trafficking of anything is not populating in our streets in those areas to hinder. Private affairs, until God makes known.

GOD IS LOVE

Remembering: Lesson Learned. Now I know why News Media 27 wanted to ask me that question relating to how I felt about the newly built Justice Court District Center. I had nothing to say bad at the time. You have to remember this was less than two years ago. This building is huge, now that I think about it. Would you believe this building is being paid for even by use? I would not be surprised if we hold a great deal of those accounts. The tapes are there; replay it if you have to. You will see me several times in you all's media. Little did I realize but I did give you the permission. Catch the shot you did of my work and I will have to say, you all are also watchers. The good thing is that is okay because I have nothing to hide. There are a lot of watchers from God so I never mind. As long as I stay on Jesus' side I am okay. One day you all tape me on film, which was the flood weekend in Lexington. I cannot remember us having one like that for a long time. I was running through that puddle of rain and enjoying it. What do you all think? I will not say because I do not have to.

Share the wealth Lexington just clean up the filthy areas around so we can move some people on to where we need to be going.

Let us welcome the newcomers to our town with better conditions than before.

There has to be a change in lawlessness turned around and it starts with us. This town used to be retired country...Too slow for the fast ones, but that is why they have big cities.

St. Matthew 27:33

They cam to a place name Golgotha, which means "Place of a Skull." 9.2.5.6.8.

Let me tell you this true short story about this buddy doing wrongs and living lawless. He at first sold illegal drugs and then got caught and went through a program in which he received a certificate after completion of the course. He appeared okay with it if you asked me. He continues to sell illegal drugs for someone else now, but is allowed. What is the certificate about? – Self-esteem if you ask me.

What type of support is that for our people, when we need to depend on there support? We can do wrong by ourselves? Do not bring it to our table. We cannot depend on you when you depend on them for they can be wrong. God is the only right – do not sell your soul cheap. It is worth more then that – God promises everlasting life if we serve him and love our selves as we would our neighbors.

Outcry, there has become a great more demand for women and children to join in and participate with the out of control lawlessness going on in this town. I cry: one woman's spirit to another, women are you ready to do jail time? That is what you will get. If you let them have their way, someone has already spoke up and thinks we need to abort our babies, can you imagine? This report has run across the television programs too much. The newspaper had an article also here recently. They are trying to keep us from our men folks. People will continue to try anything. There has never been a situation that has made me forget my maker. God wants us to multiple through his word and he will take care of us. We have to take the responsibilities with him.

Please remember in Noah's days he was instructed by God's Holy Spirit. The ark was as big as the titanic, can you image all this on faith? Noah and his family was saved because he obeyed Jehovah God. The world's become lawless again. God did not come to destroy. He has come to fulfill.

I must go now because there is still more to tell. I look forward to hearing how this will go.

Matthew 24:37

For just as the days of Noah wee, so the presence of the Son of man will be. 9.2.5.6.8.

For as they were in those days before the flood, eating and drinking, men marrying and women being given in marriage, until the day that Noah entered into the ark; and they took no note until the flood came and swept them all away, so the presence of the Son of man will be. 9.2.5.6.8.

Revelation 22:1 – 5

And he showed me a river of water of life, clear as crystal, flowing out from the throne of God and the Lamb. 9.2.5.6.8.

And no more will there be any curse. But the throne of God and of the Lamb will be in {the City], and his slaves will render him sacred service; and they will see his face and his name will be on their foreheads. 9.2.5.6.8.

And he said to me: These words are faithful and true; yes, Jehovah the God of the inspired expressions of the prophets sent his angel forth to show his slaves the things that must shortly take place. And, look! I am coming quickly. Happy is anyone observing the words of the prophecy of this scroll. 9.2.5.6.8.

Well, I John was the one hearing and seeing these things. And when I had heard and seen, I fell down to worship before the feet of the angel that had been showing me these things. But he tells me" "Be careful'! Do not do that! Worship God." 9.2.5.6.8.

He that is doing unrighteousness, let him do unrighteousness still; and let him the filthy one be made filthy still, but let the righteous one do righteous still, and let the holy one be made still. 9.2.5.6.8.

Revelation 22:16 – 21

"I, Jesus, sent my angel to bear witness to you people of these things for the congregation. I am the root and the offspring of David, and the bright morning star." 9.2.5.6.8.

And the spirit and the bride keep on saying: "Come!" And let anyone hearing say: "Come!'; And let anyone thirsting come; let anyone that wishes take life's water free. 9.2.5.6.8.

"I am bearing witness to everyone that hears the words of the prophecy of this scroll: If anyone makes an addition to these things, God will add to him the plagues that are written in this scroll; and if anyone takes anything away from the words of the scroll of this prophecy, God will take his portion away from the trees of life and out of the holy city, things which are written about in this scroll." He that bears witness of these things says, Yes; I am coming quickly? 9.2.5.6.8.

[May] the underserved kindness the Lord Jesus Christ [be] with the holy ones.

Psalms 147:4

he is counting the number of the stars, all of them he calls by their names.

Judge 5:20

from heaven did the stars fight from thier orbits they frought against sisera

Romans 1:16.

For i am not ashamed of the Good News: is in fact, God's power for salvation to everyone *having faith, to the Jew first and also to the Greek.*

Jesus loves us all, he saves those who ask to be saved thou his name. Repent, in all we do so he can show you mercy and grace through his ever loving undeserved kindness.

STORMS HIT CENTRAL KENTUCKY
Power cut, traffic snarled

LIGHTNING INJURES LEXINGTON MAN'S FOOT, STARTS FIRE IN GARAGE

HERALD-LEADER STAFF REPORT

A man was injured by lightning yesterday afternoon as storms hit Central Kentucky, knocking out power and snarling traffic.

The man was struck in the foot while working with a friend in a detached garage on Crescent Avenue. The lightning also caused a fire in the garage but was quickly put out by firefighters, said Maj. Tommy Blythe of the Lexington fire department.

The injured man, who was taken to the University of Kentucky Hospital by the other man in the garage, was treated and released, Blythe said.

The lightning storms caused power outages for 11,000 customers in Lexington, said Cliff Feltham, spokesman for Kentucky Utilities.

Many of the outages occurred from downtown out past the airport along Versailles Road, including traffic lights on Versailles, Feltham said.

"This was the first time we've had a spring storm of this magnitude," he said.

If more than 10,000 customers are affected, that is considered a high number, Feltham said.

Only 75 customers were still without power as of 10 last night, and Feltham expected that they would have power by 11.

More rain fell elsewhere in the state, said James Brotherton, meteorologist for the National Weather Service.

There were flash flood warnings in Jefferson and Oldham counties, with up to 2 inches of rain falling in an hour. Lexington received about a third of an inch, said John Denman, a meteorologist with the National

CHARLES BERTRAM | STAFF

Carla Sweat hurried across a flooded parking lot during yesterday's storm to get to work at the Lexington Center for Health and Rehabilitation on Waller Avenue.

Weather Service.

Lexington and Eastern Kentucky could experience more afternoon thunderstorms today, but the weekend should be more clear, according to the weather service.

23

REFERENCE

1. Alexandria, Virginia:"Feat and Wisdom of the Ancients" Time life books. 1990.

2. American Bible Society: "Holy Bible" New York, New York 1997.

3. Bapty-Trickey Carolyn "The Book of Of Angels" Ottenheimer Publishers. 1994.

4. Bar Charts and Company."Anatomy".

5. Crusade Bible Publishers, INC;"Holy Bible" Nashville, Tennessee.

6. Dictionary World "Holy Bible", The World Publishing Company. Cleveland, New York

7. Dictionary Webster's

8. Master Reference Edition: "Holy Bible" Heirloom Bible Publishers. 1964.

9. WatchTower Bible And Tract Society OF NY INC." New Wolrd Translation of the Holy Scriptures.1961.

10. WatchTower Bible And Tract Society OF NY INC. "Sing Praised To Jehovah. 1961

11. Various illustrated Biographical pictures from "WhoWho in the Bible". The Reader's Digest Association INC.1994.

African women her story though time Dr.Carter.

The African-American Jubilee Edition" Holy Bible" 1995.

References

Genesis
The story of creation

Genesis chapter 1:26-27. Genesis chapter 2: 7+22.
Genesis 3:13-24. Genesis 4:1-2. Genesis
Genesis 5:1-2. Genesis 9:1;6;11;12-17, Genesis 18: 25.
Genesis 22: 18. Genesis 25: 24 – 26.

Exodus
The Lord Gives Greater Power To Moses
Exodus 4:1,;12-13. Exodus 10:13;21-22. Exodus 14:1-31.
Exodus 15:1-27. Exodus 22: 16.

Leviticus

Leviticus 4:1-2;22;25;27. Leviticus 5:5. Leviticus 7: 26 –
27. Leviticus 17:10-12, 14. Leviticus 23:1-2.
Leviticus 24:22. Leviticus 26:13.

Numbers

Numbers 24:16-17.

Deuteronomy

Deuteronomy 3:1-29. Deuteronomy
4:6;12;16.Deuteronomy 5:1-22.Deuteronomy 6:1-25.
Deut 11:22-23. Deut 12:32. Deut 17:18. Deut 31:6-10. Deut 32:8-9.

Joshua

Joshua 1:9. Joshua 9:23.

Samuel

Samuel 2:9.11Samuel 22:1-51.11 Samuel 23:1-5.

1-11King

1 King 18: 1-2;44-46.King 19:11.

11 King

11King 2;9-14.11 King 3:22.11King 15:19-20;23;25.11King 20:8-10.

Job

Job 3:24. Job 7:7. Job 12:12-13. Job 14:5-22. Job 32:17-18. Job 33:1-33. Job 38:7. Job 40:14.

Psalms

Psalms 4: 1-8;18; Psalms 5:1-12. Psalms 19:8;1+14. Psalms 24:1+10. Psalms 25:15. Psalms 30:9. Psalms 33:8. Psalms 35:7. Psalms 37:25. Psalm 55:6. Psalms 50 8:2. Psalm 58:2. Psalm 68:11. Psalm 78:3-8. Psalms 86:2. Psalm 88:15. Psalms 90:1-17. Psalms 102:18. Psalms 103:5. Psalms 105: 15. Psalms 110:3. Psalms 112:4. 115: 15, 18 .Psalms 116:1-19. Psalms 118:1, 14;24. Psalms 119:1-174.

Proverbs

Proverbs 3:1; Proverbs 5: 17. Proverbs 11:12; 14; 29. Proverb 16:13. Proverbs 15: 34. Proverbs 22:6. Proverbs 29:18. Proverbs 30:6; 11. Proverbs 31:20; 26.

St. Matthews

St. Matthews 1 :1-25. St. Matthews 2: 1-23;50. St. Matthews 3 :13-17. St. Matthew 7: 24 plus 25. St. Matthews 10:7-27; St. Matthews 11: 25-30. St. Matthews 12; 39. St. Matthews 13:5;13-16. St. Matthew 17:2-3. St. Matthews 19:4-4; St. Matthew 27: 22.1-66. St. Matthews 28:1-20.

Mark\

Mark 3: 12.

Luke

Luke 2:3; Luke 4;5;6;18. Luke 6 :39. Luke 7:42. Luke
8:16. Luke 9: 48. Luke 10: 1;13;27.
Luke 11: 49. Luke 12: 1-12.35;49;50;53. Luke 13: 18.
Luke 17:24-27; Luke 24:1-53. Luke 50:1.

John

John 1:2-3;13. John 3:2-3.;4;6;17-39. John 5: 19-47.
John 5:28. John 7:42.:37-44.
John 8: 14.;31;44. John 9: 34. John 11:12;25-26. John
13: 23, 25, 28. John 14:1-31.
John 15:1;26. John 16: 13-17. John 17: 5, 26. John 18:
37. John 19:26 plus 27.

Acts

Acts 1:1-3.16,22-23. Acts 2:4;22;37;38 .Acts 3:5.
Acts 4:31;Acts 5:13;29.Acts 6;3. Acts 8:5-25.Acts 9:3,
Acts 16:19-20;30.Acts 20;24.

Timothy

Timothy 1:13. Timothy 2:14. Timothy 4:14. Timothy 11-12.
Timothy 22: 23-25.

2 Timothy

11 Timothy 1 :6;9.11. 11 Timothy 3:10-11. 11 Timothy 4:6.

Corinthians

Corinthians 6:19. Cor 7:39.Cor 12:4;12-14.Cor 15:45-49.

2 Corinthians

2 Corinthians 2:14. Cor 3:2-3. Cor11:2. Cor 12:1-20. Cor 11:2. Cor 13:1.

Galatians

Galatians 6:11.
Ephesians please read all.

Titus

Titus 3:5-8. Please read all remaining chapters.

Philippians

Philippians 1:8,19-20. Phil 3:11. Philippians 4:19.

Romans

Romans 1:16; Romans 6:4-6. Romans 8:2,3,11,15.
Romans 10:7.

Colossians

Colossians please read all chapters and verses.

1 Thessalonians

2 Thessalonians please read all chapters and verse

1 timothy/2 timothy seen above please read all remaining.

Philemon

Philemon please read all chapters and versus.

Hebrews

Hebrews 4:12;.Hebrews 9:24-28.Hebrews 10:15.
Hebrews 11:19. Hebrews 13:4. Please read all remaining chapters and verses.

James

James please read all remaining chapters and verses.

First John, second John, and third John please read all chapters and verses.

Revelation

Revelations 4:6 , please read all of Revelation's chapters and verses.

I have not had anykind of life or death situation ever occur in my life. Nor have i come close to death. What i have had is the experience of passing over from death to life. My lord has refreshed me thou miracle events from his great powers when ever i have called upon his great name he has been there to help me along. Jesus has been resurrected and his presents are here. The comforter he gives us. But God has shared with me his everloving glory. We have been made brand new, and our old ways have come to pass. This spirit knows that the time is near. This is why I'm telling the nation. Gods hands are coming back soon. Repent, and turn back from wick ways so you can have everlasting life. The Holy Bible is ful of written prophesy inspired from Gods promise to mankind. My little book is ful of stories he has promised to us believers from

11/06/2005

11/08/2005

ABOUT THE AUTHOR:

Born and rise in Lexington,Kentucky all my days and loving it. Married in the year of "82" to my high school sweetheart,who still remains the only beloved. Rise two beautiful children a daughter and son. Now with new additions a good son-in-law with six beautiful / grandchildren. Five boys and the last being a girl. Thankful, we are wealth because we are all health. God is Good. We are in our prime of life, and I must say: I'm happy. Enjoying what God has given me grandchildren,ability to work many talents,family and friends. Blessed as always, now feeling a sense of responsibly to my Lord and Savior I share the life his given me by writing the story. I plan to continue to writing the stories.